WEST
COUNTRY
LARDER

Traditional Recipes from

DORSET

Compiled by Alison Ainsworth and Yvonne Dawe

Peninsula
Press

Published by Peninsula Press
P.O. Box 31
Newton Abbot
Devon TQ12 5XH

Editorial, Design and Production:
A&B Creative Services
Kingskerswell
Devon TQ12 5EZ
Tel: 0803 873599

Sales and Distribution:
Town & Country Books
Kingskerswell
Devon TQ12 5AZ
Tel: 0803 875875

Printed in England by Penwell Ltd, Callington, Cornwall.

The publishers would like to thank the many people of Dorset who
have contributed to this book.

ISBN 1 872640 03 6

WEST COUNTRY LARDER
· DORSET ·

ᘒ Contents ᘒ

INTRODUCTION

With its rolling hills and downs and a coastline boasting the most varied geology in Europe, Dorset is one of the most beautiful counties in Britain. Farming has always been important here, not only for dairy products such as the famous Blue Vinney cheese - traditionally served with crisp rolls called Dorset Knobs - but also for sheep, cattle and a wide variety of vegetables and fruit. The Dorset Horn, a white faced sheep prized for its tender meat, frequently breeds out of season, and Lamb's Tail Pie was once a favourite dish.

Rabbit was also popular, with rabbit farming widely practised to ensure a regular supply. Tipsy Rabbit, a warming casserole of rabbit pieces simmered slowly in light ale with bacon and apples, is just as delicious as other, more expensive cuts of meat.

In common with the rest of the West Country, Dorset produces good crops of apples, with names such as Bloody Butcher, Sheep's Nose and Iron Apple, and the many cooking varieties are used to make a variety of dishes, including Blackberry and Apple Meringue Pie, a delightful concoction of fragrant fruit topped with frothy meringue.

Cider has always been a popular drink here, and another local drink, Dorset Ale, was mentioned by Thomas Hardy, the famous novelist and poet, whose stories about country life in nineteenth century 'Wessex' have absorbed generations of readers.

Soups

Savoy Cream Soup
Easy Peasy Soup
Cabbage Soup

SAVOY CREAM SOUP

Pumpkins deserve a better fate than being made into lanterns on All Hallows night, and this delicious soup will ward off any winter chills.

Ingredients
Serves 4

1lb (450g) pumpkin
2 medium leeks
2 medium potatoes
1/2 pint (275ml) milk
1/2 pint (275ml) water
2oz (50g) butter, plus a knob to finish
Salt and pepper
Chopped parsley to garnish

Method
Peel pumpkin and potatoes and cut into small cubes. Wash and slice leeks. Melt the butter in a large saucepan, add the vegetables and cook over a gentle heat for about five minutes. Add the milk and water and season to taste. Simmer, covered, for 30 minutes, then mash with a fork or put through a blender.

Add the knob of butter just before serving. Sprinkle with parsley and serve piping hot.

EASY PEASY SOUP

London is not alone in having thick fogs, or pea soupers. The undulating hills of Dorset have their fair share of mists, when the ghosts of ancient Romans can be imagined around every corner!

Ingredients
Serves 6

4oz (110g) diced bacon
4oz (110g) diced carrots
4oz (110g) diced celery
4oz (110g) chopped onions
1oz (25g) butter
1lb (450g) split dried peas, soaked
overnight in cold water
4 pints (just over 2 litres) ham stock
Sprig of mint
Salt and pepper

Method

Melt the butter in a large saucepan and fry the bacon over a gentle heat for about five minutes. Add the carrots, celery and onions and cook for a further five minutes, or until the onions become transparent. Rinse the soaked peas well under running water, then add to the pan, together with the stock and the sprig of mint. Bring to a gentle simmer and cook for about 2 ½ hours. Skim off any froth that appears.

Rub the mixture through a sieve, or liquidise in a blender. Return to the pan and heat thoroughly. Season with salt and pepper. To turn this soup into a substantial meal, add good quality frankfurter sausages cut into bite-sized pieces.

CABBAGE SOUP

Dorset has the distinction of being the first place in England to grow cultivated cabbage.

"Take a large cabbage, chopped, one large onion, sliced, four sticks of celery, washed and sliced, and a crushed clove of garlic. Put these in a large saucepan together with some streaky bacon, ham, and half a pound of dried peas which have been soaked overnight. Add two pints of boiling water and simmer for four hours. Season with salt and pepper and add a dash of vinegar just before serving."

Traditional

Meat & Fish

Lyme Bay Haddock Casserole

Red Mullet

Magog Mackerel

Long Puddle Lamb

Lamb's Tail Pie

Tipsy Rabbit

Puddle Bacon Cake

Rooky Pie

Dorset Casserole with Dumplings

Dorset Sausage

Dorset Jugged Steak

To Dress Beef Steaks

To Draw Gravey

Sorrel Purée

LYME BAY HADDOCK CASSEROLE

Good fresh fish is readily available in Dorset, and this recipe is equally good using either haddock or cod.

Ingredients
Serves 2-3

1lb (450g) haddock or cod fillet
8oz (225g) tomatoes, peeled and sliced
2oz (50g) button mushrooms, sliced
1 medium onion, chopped
1 tablespoon chopped parsley
1/4 pint (150ml) cider
2 tablespoons fresh white breadcrumbs
2oz (50g) grated Cheddar cheese
Salt and freshly ground black pepper

Method

Skin the fish and cut into cubes. Put the fish in a casserole, cover with the tomatoes, mushrooms and onion, then sprinkle with the parsley and seasonings. Pour over the cider, cover and bake at 180°C (350°F) gas mark 4, for 20-25 minutes or until the fish is cooked. Mix together the breadcrumbs and cheese, and sprinkle on top of the fish. Place under a hot grill until the cheese and breadcrumbs are golden brown.

RED MULLET

Sometimes called the 'woodcock of the sea', because like the game bird of that name it is better cooked with its liver intact.

Ingredients
Serves 2

2 red mullet
2oz (50g) breadcrumbs
2oz (50g) melted butter
1 teaspoon chopped fennel
2 teaspoons chopped parsley
Juice of half a lemon
Salt and pepper

Method

Cut off head, tail and fins or ask your fishmonger to do it for you. Score the fish on both sides. Butter a shallow ovenproof dish, place the fish in it, then sprinkle with salt, pepper, parsley, fennel and lemon juice. Pour over the melted butter, cover with foil and bake at 180°C (350°F) gas mark 4 for 20 minutes, basting several times during cooking.
Serve with a green salad and wholemeal bread.

MAGOG MACKEREL

A wide variety of fish is to be found in the sea off the Dorset coast, including bass, black bream, cod, dab, flounder, garfish, mullet, plaice, sole, whiting and of course mackerel, which is probably the most prolific, and which needs only simple cooking.

Ingredients
Serves 4

4 medium mackerel
8oz (225g) gooseberries
2oz (50g) butter
3 tablespoons breadcrumbs
Salt and black pepper

Method

Top, tail and clean the mackerel, and do the same with the gooseberries. Heat and soften the gooseberries in the butter over a low heat until slightly mushy. Allow to cool slightly, then add salt, pepper and breadcrumbs to make a manageable stuffing.

Open the mackerel, lay it skin side up and press firmly with your thumbs down the back to loosen the bone. Turn the fish over and lift the backbone away from the flesh. Divide the stuffing into four and fill each fish. Close the fish and lay in a well buttered ovenproof dish. Cover with foil and bake at 180°C (350°F) gas mark 4 for 30 minutes. Serve with crusty bread, Dorset butter and a green salad.

LONG PUDDLE LAMB

The Dorset Horn is a white faced sheep which is valued worldwide, both for its tender meat and its medium length wool. Some of the ewes breed out of season and the lambs grow rapidly in the lush green Dorset meadows.

Ingredients
Serves 4-6

1 ½lb (700g) leg or shoulder of lamb, boned
2 ½oz (60g) butter
2 small onions
1 clove garlic
2 tablespoons Worcestershire sauce
2 tablespoons chopped parsley
1/4 pint (150ml) stock
1/4 pint (150ml) cider
Flour, salt and pepper

Method

Cut the meat into cubes and coat with seasoned flour. Peel and chop the onion and crush the garlic. Heat the butter in a large, heavy-based saucepan and brown the meat in it. Transfer the meat to a casserole together with the onion, garlic and parsley. Add the stock and cider to the juices in the saucepan and stir until boiling. Now add the Worcestershire sauce and seasoning and simmer for 5 minutes. Pour over the meat, cover and cook in a preheated oven at 190°C (375°F) gas mark 5 for an hour or until tender.

Serve with plain boiled potatoes and vegetables. This dish can be cooked in advance as it reheats very well.

LAMB'S TAIL PIE

No Dorset feast would have been complete without this tasty pie.

"Take lambs' tails from Dorset Horns and put them in a pie dish with some bacon, hard boiled eggs, fresh herbs, lemon peel and seasoning. Pour over some stock and cover with pastry."

Traditional

TIPSY RABBIT

Rabbit was once the staple diet of country folk, and in addition to the wild variety, rabbit farming was also widely practised, hence the proliferation of 'Warren Inns' throughout the county.

Ingredients
Serves 4

1 ½lb (700g) rabbit pieces
6oz (175g) bacon, chopped
2 medium onions, peeled and chopped
1 cooking apple, cored and sliced
8 stoned prunes
1 medium carrot, chopped
1 celery stalk, chopped
1/2 pint (275ml) light beer
Salt and pepper
Nutmeg

Method

Fry the bacon until the fat runs. Transfer to casserole and fry the rabbit pieces in the bacon fat until lightly browned on all sides. Place on top of the bacon. Now fry onions and apple until golden but not browned. Add to casserole, together with the prunes, carrot, celery and beer. Season with salt, pepper and freshly grated nutmeg.

Cover and cook in a preheated oven at 170°C (325°F) gas mark 3 for 1½-2 hours or until the meat is tender. Serve with parsley potatoes and minty peas.

PUDDLE BACON CAKE

This was originally known as 'Piddle Bacon Cake', after the River Piddle, but the name was changed to Puddle, to spare the blushes of Victorian cooks!

Ingredients
Serves 4

1 ½lb (700g) minced lean bacon
1 ½oz (40g) butter
2 ½oz (60g) soft brown sugar
1 tablespoon minced onion
2 large pineapple rings
2 slightly beaten eggs
2oz (50g) stale breadcrumbs
4 Maraschino cherries
10 whole cloves
1/2 teaspoon mustard powder
1/4 teaspoon black pepper

Method

Melt the butter and dissolve the sugar in it. Use this mixture to cover the base of a round 7" (18cm) cake tin. Cut the pineapple rings into wedges and place in a decorative pattern over the base of the cake tin. Mix the remaining ingredients until thoroughly blended, spread over pine-apple base, press down firmly, stud with cloves and bake in a moderate oven 180°C (350°F) gas mark 4 for 1 hour.

Remove cloves and turn 'cake' onto a large heated platter and decorate the top with cherries. Surround the base of the platter with watercress.

ROOKY PIE

The 'good olde days' were not so good for villagers who had to exist on very low wages, or in some cases no wages at all. Food was obtained from whatever sources were available.

"Take four good rooks, pluck them, chop off the heads and feet, and cut into four pieces each. Put in a large pie dish with some veal, bacon and stock, and cover with a pastry lid. Bake for one hour. Serve with caution."

Traditional

DORSET CASSEROLE WITH DUMPLINGS

Ingredients
Serves 4

1lb (450g) lean braising steak
1 medium onion, chopped
2oz (50g) mushrooms, sliced
8oz (225g) carrots, diced

8oz (225g) turnips, diced
1 tablespoon cooking oil
1 tablespoon plain flour
1/2 pint (275ml) good quality beef stock
1/4 pint (150ml) cider
Salt and pepper

Method

Heat the oil in a flameproof casserole or heavy frying pan. Cut the meat into 2" (5cm) cubes and brown thoroughly in the oil. Remove from the pan, using a slotted spoon. Add the vegetables to the pan and cook over a low heat for 5-7 minutes, stirring occasionally. Stir in the flour and continue cooking gently, stirring constantly, for two minutes. Remove from the heat and gradually whisk in the cider and stock. Return pan to the heat and bring to the boil, stirring constantly. Add the meat to the casserole and season to taste. Cover and cook in a preheated oven at 180°C (350°F) gas mark 4, for 2 hours or until the meat is tender.

Ingredients for the dumplings

4oz (110g) self raising flour
2oz (50g) beef or vegetable suet
1 tablespoonful chopped parsley
Milk to mix
Salt and pepper

Method

Mix together the flour, suet, parsley, salt and pepper and stir in enough milk to make a firm dough. Shape into 12 even-sized balls with floured hands. Approximately 25 minutes before the end of the cooking time remove the casserole from the oven, stir well and adjust the seasoning. Place the dumplings on top of the meat, and return the casserole to the oven, uncovered, for the remainder of the cooking time.

DORSET SAUSAGE

This isn't a sausage at all, but a coarse terrine, or meat loaf. It makes an ideal dish for a picnic or cold supper and is best made the day before it is eaten.

Ingredients
Serves 8

1lb (450g) minced beef
1lb (450g) minced ham or bacon
6oz (175g) fresh breadcrumbs
2 tablespoons chopped parsley
2 eggs
2 teaspoons Worcestershire sauce
1/2teaspoon ground mace
1/2 nutmeg, grated
Salt and pepper

Method

Mix the beef and ham or bacon in a bowl together with the breadcrumbs. Beat the eggs then stir into the meat mixture and add the spices and seasoning. Make sure everything is well blended then grease a large oblong cake tin and spoon the mixture into it. Cover the top with foil and place the tin in a roasting tin containing 1-2" (2-5cm) warm water. Bake in a preheated oven at 170°C (325°F) gas mark 3 for 1½ hours.

Remove from oven, then leave overnight to get completely cold. Turn out of the tin and decorate with sliced pickled gherkins. Cut into thick slices and serve with toast and salad.

DORSET JUGGED STEAK

A rich beef casserole which has the 'jugged' flavour associated with hare. The sausagemeat balls are also excellent with game or as a stuffing for chicken or turkey. Very filling!

Ingredients
Serves 4-6

2lb (900g) shin of beef
1 large onion
1/4 pint (150ml) stock
2 tablespoons port or red wine (optional)
2 teaspoons redcurrant jelly
4 cloves
1 teaspoon dried mixed herbs
Flour, salt and pepper
Beef dripping or oil

Ingredients for the meat balls

8oz (225g) sausagemeat
1 cup breadcrumbs
1 egg
Salt and pepper

Method
Cut the beef into cubes, roll in seasoned flour and fry lightly on both sides in dripping or oil. Transfer to a large ovenproof casserole and add the chopped onion, stock and red wine if used. Top up with water, if necessary, to just cover. Add cloves, mixed herbs and seasoning, stir well and cover. Cook in a preheated oven at 150°C (300°F) gas mark 2 for about 2 hours, checking occasionally to see that the liquid has not run dry. Top up with stock or water as required.

Method for the meat balls

Mix together the sausagemeat, breadcrumbs and beaten egg, and season with salt and pepper. With floured hands, divide the mixture into a number of walnut-sized balls. Poach in boiling water for 5-10 minutes, removing any scum as it forms. Drain and set aside.

When the casserole is thoroughly cooked, stir in the redcurrant jelly and add the sausagemeat balls. Return the casserole, uncovered, to the oven for a further 10 minutes.
Serve with potatoes baked in their jackets and carrots.

TO DRESS BEEF STAKES

"Take goode buttock beef & cut it in thin slices, & chop it as you doe for Scotch Scollops wash them all over with Eggs on both sides & strew them over pretty thick with Crumbs of bread mixt with sweet herbs, a little pepper & salt, fry them with very little liquor for the sauce take a little Gravy, Anchovy, & butter, & Lemon if you please . . ."

From a 17th century Receipt Book.

TO DRAW GRAVEY

"Take some slices of buttock Beife hack it with ye back of a Knife put it into a frying pan fry them with a little fresh butter just enough to brown then put in a pint of water an oynion a bunch of sweet hearbs a little whole pepper & 2 or 3 anchovies so let it stew leisurely over ye fire till half ye licquor is wasted then squeese out the juce of ye meat between 2 trenchers and keep it for your use . . ."

From a 17th century Receipt Book.

SORREL PURÉE

"Sorrel sharpens the appetite assuages heat, cools the liver, and strengthens the heart . . ."

John Evelyn 1699

In addition to being served as a vegetable or in soups sorrel was also used as a purgative and as a cure for toothache. Farm workers chewed its leaves to quench their thirst.

French sorrel has tender young leaves with a lemony flavour that makes a delicious accompaniment for chicken, ham, white fish or eggs.

Ingredients
Serves 4

2lb (900g) sorrel
2 eggs
1/4 pint (150ml) double cream
1 1oz (40g) butter
1/4 teaspoon grated nutmeg
Salt and pepper

Method
Wash and chop the sorrel. Melt the butter in a large heavy based pan, and cook the sorrel, covered, for about 5 minutes until tender. Remove the lid and add the cream and the eggs, beaten. Season with salt and pepper and simmer gently, uncovered, stirring frequently, until the mixture thickens. Do not allow to come to the boil. Serve sprinkled with nutmeg.

Cakes & Puddings

Sweetheart Cake

Blackmore Vale Cake

Blackberry and Apple Meringue Pie

Golden Cap Pudding

Apple Frumenty

Rennet

Wessex Junket

SWEETHEART CAKE

Wishing wells are frequently to be found in Dorset, and many a hopeful lad or lass sat by one and recited this sweet little couplet on Midsummer's Eve.

"Hoping this night
My truelove to see,
I place my shoes
In the form of a T."

Ingredients

2oz (50g) butter
4oz (110g) sugar
8oz (225g) plain flour
2 eggs
2oz (50g) chopped almonds
1 teaspoon baking powder
8oz (225g) sifted icing sugar
Ratafia essence
Water
Crystallised or fresh roses

Method

Cream butter and sugar until soft, then beat in the eggs one at a time. Sieve the flour and baking powder and stir into the mixture. Add the chopped almonds. Transfer to a buttered cake tin (heart shaped if you have one) and bake in a preheated oven at 180°C (350°F) gas mark 4 for about 50 minutes. Remove from the tin after 10 minutes and allow to cool on a wire rack. When cold cover with water icing made with the icing sugar, ratafia essence and water, and decorate with crystallised or fresh roses.

BLACKMORE VALE CAKE

This cake has been eaten by the Blackmore Vale Hunt for over 100 years.

Ingredients

4oz (110g) butter
4oz (110g) caster sugar
12oz (350g) plain flour
12oz (350g) raisins
3oz (75g) chopped mixed peel
1 teaspoon bicarbonate of soda
2 teaspoons golden syrup
1/4pt (150ml) milk

Method

Cream together the butter and sugar. Heat the milk and dissolve the bicarbonate of soda and syrup in it. Add the sieved flour gradually to the butter and sugar mixture, alternately with the milk mixture, beating well. Stir in the raisins and chopped mixed peel. Transfer to a lined and greased 6" (15cm) cake tin and bake in the centre of a preheated oven at 180°C (350°F) gas mark 4 for 2½ hours.

BLACKBERRY AND APPLE MERINGUE PIE

Orchards and hedgerows flourish in Dorset and you can combine a delightful walk with gathering the ingredients for this unusual pudding.

Ingredients

8oz (225g) shortcrust pastry
3 Bramley cooking apples
8oz (225g) blackberries
4oz (110g) brown sugar
Pinch of ground cloves
2 egg whites
3 tablespoons sifted icing sugar
2-3 tablespoons water

Method

Line a pie dish with the shortcrust pastry and bake blind at the top of a preheated oven at 200°C (400°F) gas mark 6 for 10 minutes. Reset the oven to 170°C (325°F) gas mark 3. Peel, core and slice the apples and simmer gently together with the blackberries, sugar, ground cloves and the water until softened. Leave to cool for about 10 minutes, before spooning the mixture carefully onto the pastry base. Beat the egg whites until they form stiff peaks, then fold in the icing sugar and continue beating until glossy. Spoon the meringue over the pie and return to the middle of the oven for 20 minutes.

GOLDEN CAP PUDDING

If you can bear to leave the pretty highway through Chideock, take the sea road to the beach called Seatown. Here in all its glory you will see the beautiful rising cliff face known as Golden Cap.

Ingredients

6oz (175g) self-raising flour
4oz (110g) soft margarine

WEST COUNTRY LARDER · DORSET

4oz (110g) caster sugar
2 lightly beaten eggs
2 tablespoons marmalade
Finely grated rind and juice of one large orange

Method

Spread the marmalade in the base of a buttered 2 pint (1.1 litre) pudding basin. Sift the flour into a mixing bowl and add the sugar, margarine and eggs. Beat for 2-3 minutes until the mixture is light and fluffy, add the orange juice and rind and blend thoroughly together. Spoon the mixture into the basin and cover the top with greased foil, pleated in the centre to allow the pudding to rise during steaming. Secure with string. Place in a large saucepan containing enough boiling water to reach halfway up the sides of the basin. Cover and steam for 2 hours, topping up with more water as necessary. Do not allow to boil dry. Allow to cool slightly before turning out onto a serving dish. Serve with single cream.

APPLE FRUMENTY

This is a more palatable version of the 'furmity' sold to country folk visiting the fairs that came annually to the West Country. Indeed it was 'furmity' laced with rum that led to the dreadful deed of the Mayor of Casterbridge, in Thomas Hardy's novel.

Ingredients

4 large Bramley cooking apples
4oz (110g) dark muscovado sugar
1/4 pint (150ml) cider
1/4 pint (150ml) water
1/2 teaspoon powdered cinnamon
Toasted almonds for topping

Method

Peel, core and slice the apples and place in a saucepan together with the sugar, cinnamon, cider and water. Cook until soft and mushy. Turn into a bowl, sprinkle toasted almonds on top, and serve with a thin pouring custard or single cream.

RENNET

"Let the calf suck as much as he will, just before he is killed. Take the milk bag out of the calf and let it lie 12 hours covered with stinging nettles till it is red. Then take out your curd and wash the bag clean and salt it inside and out. Let it lie in salt for 24 hours, then wash your curd in new milk and clean it and put it back in the bag with 3 or 4 streakings [the last milk from the cow], a beaten egg, 10 cloves, a blade of mace, and skewer the bag shut and hang in a pot.

In another pot put 1/2 pint of salted water, 5 tops of the reddish blackthorn, the same of burnet, 3 of sweet marjoram and boil altogether, let it cool, then put some of this flavoured water into the bag with the egg and milk and let the bag soak in the rest of it. This in which the bag lies (and into which the heavier liquid from inside the bag exudes) is the rennet, and it is so strong that the bag can be refilled and left to exude more than 6 or 7 times before the curdling action of the stomach juice is exhausted."

From a 16th century recipe.

WESSEX JUNKET

Fortunately we can now buy rennet in a bottle, and the simple dish of junket was frequently used as a test of skill at agricultural shows. The ideal temperature for the milk was as it came straight from the cow, a practice that would be greatly frowned upon nowadays.

Ingredients

1/2 pint (275ml) milk
1/2 pint (275ml) Dorset cream
1 ⅓oz (40g) caster sugar
1 teaspoon rennet
Nutmeg

Method

Mix the milk and cream together in a saucepan and sprinkle in the sugar. Warm this slowly until the sugar has dissolved and the milk is no more than blood heat. Stir in the rennet, pour immediately into a large shallow serving dish, and leave in a cool place to set. Do not refrigerate. Before serving, grate nutmeg evenly over the surface.

Drinks

Dorset Claret Cup
Almond Shrub
Mulled Ale
Ginger Beer

DORSET CLARET CUP

Ingredients

1 bottle light claret
1 bottle soda water
1 wine glass pounded sugar
1 large glass sherry
1 small glass curacao
The thinly pared rind of a lemon
Slices of cucumber
Sprigs of mint or borage

Method

Simply combine the first six ingredients in a glass punchbowl and garnish with slices of cucumber and sprigs of mint or borage. Chill before serving.

ALMOND SHRUB

"Take 3 gallons of rum or brandy, 3 quarts of orange juice, the peel of 3 lemons, 3lb of loaf sugar, then 4oz of bitter almonds, blanch and beat them fine, mix them all well together, let it stand an hour to curdle, run it through a flannel bag several times till it is clear, then bottle for use."

Traditional recipe

MULLED ALE

Ingredients

3 eggs
1 pint (570ml) ale
4oz (110g) caster sugar
2 pints (1.1 litre) milk
1/4 nutmeg, grated

Method

Bring the ale to the boil in a saucepan. Remove from the heat, beat the eggs well and stir into the milk. Add the ale, sugar and nutmeg and heat slowly, stirring constantly until the mixture thickens. Do not allow to boil. Pour into a jug and stir for 2 minutes.

GINGER BEER

This was a popular drink amongst country folk, especially farm workers at harvest time.

Ingredients
Makes one gallon (4.5 litres)

1oz (25g) root beer
1lb (450g) sugar
1 large lemon
1oz (25g) cream of tartar
1oz (25g) fresh yeast
8 pints (4.5 litres) boiling water

Method
Bruise the ginger by wrapping it in a cloth and hitting it with a steak tenderiser or hammer. This helps to release the flavour.

Peel the rind thinly from the lemon, then squeeze out the juice. Put the ginger, sugar, lemon rind and cream of tartar into a two gallon (9 litre) plastic bucket, then add the boiling water and the lemon juice. Stir well and leave to cool to 21°C (70°F). Cream the yeast to a smooth paste with a little warm water and stir it into the mixture. Cover the bucket with a clean cloth and secure with string or rubber bands. Leave in a warm place for 24 hours to ferment.

Skim off the froth and, being careful not to disturb the sediment, ladle the beer into clean, strong bottles, with the aid of a funnel if necessary. Cork the bottles, securing the corks with string or fine wire. Store the bottles in a cool place and keep an eye on them. The ginger beer should be ready to drink in 3-4 days, but the wires or string may need to be adjusted as the beer continues to ferment and pressure builds up.